To my good friend ??? who
shared my interest in Northern Europe
for the full wine innings!

[signature]

DENMARK

A PHOTOGRAPHER'S ODYSSEY

Marshall H. Cohen

Library of Congress Control Number: 2015902528
Big Marsh Photography, Publisher
Designed by: Maureen Donelan

Printed in Denmark by Narayana Press

In honor of the memory
of my dearest friend,
Gunnar Holm

DENMARK

A PHOTOGRAPHER'S ODYSSEY

Marshall H. Cohen

TABLE OF CONTENTS

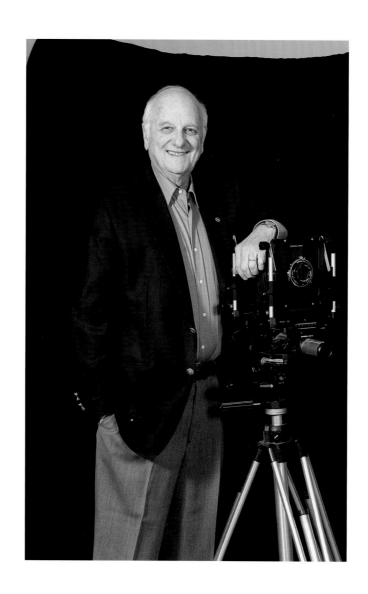

About Marshall

Marshall H. Cohen began his professional photography career as a stringer for Reuters International in Washington, D.C., eventually going on to serve as the Washington representative for Pan American News, a stock agency supplying images to Latin America. Marshall worked as a as photographer at several D.C. embassies, including Denmark, Sweden and Austria, and many corporate clients, private foundations and associations. Marshall covered the White House during the presidencies of George H. W. Bush and Bill Clinton, and worked as a staff photographer for a number of newspapers, including *The Washington Citizen* and *The Sun Scandinavia*. His photographs have been published in many National and European magazines, such as the *Washingtonian, Politiken* and *Billet Bladet*. Marshall is a member of the White House News Photographers Association, Professional Photographers of America and the National Press Club, where he founded the club's photography committee and served as its chairman for five years. He has won more than 100 awards in amateur competitions and was a national first place prize winner in a competition sponsored by British Airlines honoring Israel's 25th anniversary. He also was awarded the Nan Tracy '46 Award in 2010, an annual recognition given by the Brown University Alumni Association to distinguished graduates. Marshall is a Board Vice President of the American Scandinavian Association in Washington, D.C. and an Honorary Life Member of the Association of the Tall Ship the *Danmark*. He and his wife live in Washington, D.C.

6.

Preface and Acknowledgments

Although Denmark is often associated with its romantic 18th and 19th-century periods, partly due to its world-renowned painters and writers, the perception that Denmark is a utopian society straight out of a Hans Christian Andersen fable is outdated. Denmark today is a high-tech country powered by sophisticated windmills, driverless trains weaving in and around Copenhagen, 21st-century architecture, including a modern opera house, and world-class restaurants. Any visitor will enjoy the beauty and romance of Denmark's past—as I do—while traveling through this friendly and beautiful, modern country. I hope this book adds a modern layer to Denmark's historic past and landscapes.

One often hears Danish spokesmen, politicians and others describing Denmark with the humble truism that Denmark is a small country, its population only about six million souls, and the total land area (excluding Greenland) only 16,621 square miles. Although the country is small when compared to nearly all others in Western Europe, its history is remarkably complex. I have pieced together a photographic story of Danish history in hope that you will share my fascination with Denmark's storied past through my lens. With no fewer than 57 monarchs since Gorm the Old (958-986 A.D.), each ruler presents their own interesting story. This brief introductory history provides information about the most important members of the cast, while each photograph's caption adds further details about this country's rich culture and history.

I particularly want to thank Maureen Donelan for her creative design and patience in preparing this book. I also am grateful to my friends Dr. Rose Marie Oster, Chair of the Dept. of Scandinavian Studies, University of Maryland, and Ambassador Eric Fiil of the Danish Ministry of Foreign Affairs (Ret.), who offered enlightened criticism and historic perspective to the text. I want to thank the staff of the Danish Embassy, Washington, D.C., and particularly Jette R. Elkjaer, Cultural Advisor, for their assistance during the publication process. Others whose friendship and encouragement energized this project were author and friend Miles Lambert-Gocs (*The Wines of Greece*); Captain Kurt Andersen, Skipper of the *Danmark*; Niels J. Bagge, Director of Maritime Education (Ret.) in Denmark; and Marie Praestegaard, for her generous hospitality in Denmark. My wife Arlene was an indispensable partner in this venture, adding editorial skills as well as unending emotional support. This book honors the memory of my dearest friend Gunnar Holm who, in 1959, planted the seed that eventually blossomed into a book.

8.

Introduction: "The Curtain Rises"

My first of many visits to Denmark began in 1959, an add-on to a grand tour of Europe—an escape from a mundane job dusting and delivering furniture in my father's store in Pawtucket, Rhode Island. I was an impressionable young college graduate from Brown University with every expectation that after a ten-week escape to Europe I would return as a highly motivated merchant, ready to steer Cohen's Furniture to greatness in that small, once-renowned textile manufacturing center. Denmark changed all that.

I arrived in Copenhagen from Paris on a late September afternoon with no reservations and carrying a heavy suitcase with no wheels, wearing a feathered Austrian green felt hat, and an inexpensive plastic camera bag containing my reliable Contaflex camera. The Danish Tourist Office graciously arranged for me to stay with a local family, part of a "Meet the Danes" program. The address was 4-A Lykkeholms Alle, and I naively believed it would be a short walk from Central Station. Taking a taxi was beyond both my budget and my values. A friendly looking older gentleman approached after seeing me struggling with a tourist map and offered help. He walked me clear around a very long block, which surrounded Copenhagen's historic Tivoli Park, right back to where we started. When I pointed this out he laughed and said he merely decided this was an opportunity to practice his English and pointed out the nearest bus stop to take me down Vesterbrogade and near to my destination. This was my first experience with a local Dane—friendly, good-humored, willing to help, and a convincing good Samaritan!

My hosts were the Holm family: Gunnar, Ingeborg, and their beautiful daughter Karen. Each morning I was treated to a fine Danish breakfast of Europe's most delicious coffee in a Wedgwood coffee pot and freshly baked rolls and cheeses. The bed had a warm and cozy *duntaeppe* (quilt). I had found heaven. Gunnar was a salesman for the Toms Chocolade Factory and an amateur archeologist. For years following my return home, I received letters from Gunnar describing archeological sites he had visited while on sales trips around Denmark. His letters and warm friendship initiated my long enthusiasm for all things Danish. It is appropriate that I dedicate this book to the memory of my dear old friend Gunnar.

I returned home to Rhode Island with a renewed enthusiasm for our family store and ordered shipments of the well-know Holmsgaard Glass and the Kay Bojesen wooden soldiers. These decorated the windows of the store and prompted long conversations about Denmark with customers but sales were meager as the merchandise was a bit too upscale for Pawtucket's largely blue-collar citizens. I enrolled at Georgetown

University graduate school and received a Master of Arts in Economics, writing my thesis on post-war inflation in Denmark. My interest in Denmark, combined with a specialization in economics, qualified me to be hired as an analyst in the U.S. Department of Agriculture, eventually becoming responsible for the four Nordic countries with the department's International Division of the Economic Research Service. My interest in photography continued on an amateur level, and I chaired a seminar called "The Photographic Round-table" at the department's Graduate School while working on trade and policy issues related to agricultural and economic issues in Northern Europe.

My work with the Department of Agriculture brought me to Denmark on numerous occasions and my ever-present camera was at work even on state visits. Business appointments were primarily at Denmark's highly prestigious universities in Copenhagen and Aarhus, as well as to the many departments within the Danish Ministry of Agriculture and the Danish Ministry of Foreign Affairs. I authored several publications dealing with Danish agriculture and wrote numerous articles for the USDA weekly publication, *Foreign Agriculture*, often illustrated with my photographs. My association with the Danish Embassy in Washington, D.C. led to many "moonlighting" assignments, including Royal visits. I was the official U.S. photographer during the first visit of Crown Prince Frederick, heir to the throne.

It was during an assignment on the Danish tall ship the *Danmark* in Washington, D.C., in 1985 that I met the ship's legendary captain, Vilhelm Hansen. I was extremely humbled when he called me later in the year and told me he valued my coverage of the ship so much that he wanted me to be the official photographer on board the *Danmark* during the Parade of Tall Ships in New York in 1986. I sailed on the *Danmark* for six days along with guests Victor Borge and the celebrated U.S. journalist Walter Cronkite.

A collection of 50 photographs were given to Denmark from this experience and exhibited in museums in Denmark, including a gallery on Langelinie Prominade not far from the famous statue of the Little Mermaid. This experience was game changing, and I decided to close the 25-year chapter of my life with USDA, dust off all my cameras, and start a new journey into photojournalism.

Thank you Denmark. Enjoy my photographic odyssey.

Marshall H. Cohen, 2015

Jogging Through Danish History

May or September is my favorite month for visiting Denmark. If the weather cooperates the sky may be a dark blue, dotted with pillowy white clouds adding a delicate contrast as they glide above the copper-green spires of Copenhagen. If visitors are fortunate, there is a strong chance they will enjoy the sensual aromas of fresh pastries, fresh flowers, and roasting coffees, and other poetic experiences while traveling through Denmark, recently polled as one of the happiest countries on earth. Nevertheless, Danish history is like that of other Nordic countries—comparable to a political Rubik's Cube, its pieces carefully twisted and turned over centuries until boundaries were sealed and the present constitutional monarchy formed. This short history may add some perspective to the difficult challenges that the land of Denmark experienced beneath those fleeting beautiful skyscapes.

Over the centuries there were many wars between Denmark and Germany, Sweden, and England, all with complex alliances and military objectives. During its long history Denmark also struggled with rivalries between various internal power groups such as the royals, nobles, church leaders, and peasants, as well as resolving questions of land ownership between the Church and the monarchy. Denmark's many wars defined its boundaries and its role in Europe. The complex Schlesvig-Holstein issue alone played out over hundreds of years. For this reason, and my reminder that I am a photographer and not a historian, I am supplying a bibliography that adds a bit more historic detail than provided by my "through the lens" observations. Let's begin after the most recent Ice Age with those famous Danish Norsemen, the Vikings!

One Viking-inspired custom in Denmark is to begin a meal, or a gathering of friends, with a "snaps," a strong, intoxicating beverage called aquavit that is made from distilled potatoes and various herbs or flavorings. Beer and mead were the drinks of choice for Vikings, not snaps. The traditional Danish drinking custom is for two or more parties to clink their snaps glasses and say,

"Skal!" while making eye contact. "Skal" is an old Danish word for "skull" and originates from the Viking custom of using the skull of the enemy for a drinking vessel.

The word "snaps" is related to the Germanic "schnapps," which means any alcoholic beverage. The custom may have begun even before the established Viking period (8th to 11th century A.D.) when communities were carefully carved out along the waterways of the Nordic lands, and prior to the period when the nation states of Denmark, Norway, or Sweden began.

Vikings are remembered for their explorations, pagan rituals and lootings of English, Scottish, and Irish monasteries. However, they also were skilled farmers, expert ship builders, and practiced a unique community-based system of jurisprudence.

Denmark, geologically, is a young country. When Moses was leading the Israelites out of Egypt about 3,500 years ago, Denmark was in its Bronze Age—still a few thousand years before the Vikings. Americans' early impressions of Vikings may have been popularized in the 1958 film, "The Vikings," with romantic movie idols Kirk Douglas and Tony Curtis clashing swords and slaughtering any enemy standing between them and whatever was perceived as having value. Vikings could not have looked even vaguely like Hollywood's well-groomed actors, but there were some accurate aspects to the film. Vikings did leave their small farms and fishing communities along the coasts and waterways of Norway, Denmark, and Sweden on their long, sleek vessels seeking gold, silver, various wares and slaves. Scholars offer a variety of reasons as to why they would set out on long boats, hugging the shores wherever possible and using the stars and coastal landmarks as navigational guides to far off destinations. Whatever the reason—slaves, curiosity, famine, wives or loot— their routes were well-documented. Although Vikings from all the northern countries explored the same destinations, it appears the Danes sailed primarily to England, Scotland, and France; the Norwegians to Iceland, Greenland, and Ireland; and the Swedes to Russia and southern destinations as far as Byzantium (Constantinople).

Two aquavit "snaps" glasses: on the left, a conventional glass and on the right a stemless glass requiring the drinker to finish the toast before inverting the glass into its container.

Lets begin with Rollo, or Rolf, an early Viking chieftain born around 846 A.D. It has been established he was born in the small fishing and farming community on the small island of Giske, off the west coast of Norway near Alesund. Rollo might have been either Norwegian or Danish. During the period when he led major Viking expeditions into the Seine River basin, near Paris, Bayeux and Rouen, the French King Louis the Pious called the invaders "Norsemen" or "Northmen." He eventually settled in Normandy (named for the "Northmen"). To stop the raids, King Louis' son, Charles the Bald, appeased Rollo with gifts of revenue and a dukedom. Rollo became the first Duke of Normandy around 911 and established a Viking center in Rouen populated largely by Danish Northmen. Rollo converted to Christianity when he was baptized in 912, and the Viking population was gradually absorbed into French culture.

Reconstructed home of a Viking chief in Borg, Norway. Viking communities were settled near farmland and waterways and often with the protection of nearby mountains

The large number of Viking place names, light-haired Frenchmen, and DNA samples may establish evidence of the ties between today's Normans and yesterday's Vikings. One celebrity Viking settler from the north included Rollo's great, great, great-grandson, William the Conqueror

A significant period in Danish history was around 950 when King Gorm's son Harald Bluetooth conquered all of Norway and Denmark. Harald was baptized in Germany and the Danes slowly became Christianized. The Danish conversion event is commemorated at Jelling, Jutland, at the Jelling Church and Stone, a World Heritage site. The inscription on the large runic stone reads, "Harald King had this stone made after Gorm his father and after Thyra his mother. That Harald which conquered all Denmark and Norway and made the Danes Christians." King Gorm, following a succession of many pagan kings, is recognized as the first of a continuing bloodline of all the subsequent Danish Royals, the longest unbroken monarchy in Europe.

Harald Bluetooth returned to Denmark along with a French Benedictine monk, Saint Ansgar (801-865). Ansgar anchored Christianity in Danish soil under orders from The French King Louis the Pious, and established bishoprics and important cathedrals at Ribe (in Jutland), Lund (in Sweden) and significant locations in Germany, including Bremen.

During the late 10th and early 11th century, Viking kings "wore two helmuts," that of conquering colonizers and another of cross-bearing Christians gradually adopting the new Catholic faith of the Roman Empire within Nordic boundaries and beyond. Bluetooth's son Svend Forkbeard ruled from 985 to 1014 in parts of northeastern England under the jurisdiction of a Viking legal system called Danelaw. Svend was succeeded by his son Canute the Great (1018-1035). Canute continued to benefit from receiving a form of gratuity paid by the English to the Vikings called "Danegeld," not to be confused with the so-called "Daneverke," which was an older protective boundary constructed to mark the German-Danish northern border at that time. Canute the Great became the King of England as well as Denmark, and following the "timely" death of the Norwegian king, added Norway to his real estate portfolio. Later a second Canute assumed the throne, Canute the Holy (1080-1086), so named since his major hobby was creating convents and favoring the church with financial aid paid from heavy taxation. When he threatened to embark on more Viking raids on English soil, the heavily taxed Danish peasants had enough, followed him to Saint Albans Church in Odense and slew him on the alter.

The gradual end of the Viking period ran parallel with the absorption of Viking settlers by France, Germany, and England, and the conversion of Viking kings to Christianity, who were frequently tempted by the riches, political power and land which came with conversion. By the beginning of the 12th century, the Viking period was technically over, although one might argue that Viking customs and elements of their pagan traditions lived on.

The so-called Valdemar Period began with Valdemar I (the Great) who ruled from 1157 to1182 to Valdemar III, (called Atterdag, "the next day") king from 1340 to 1375. The Valdemar period saw great changes in Danish institutions and culture. Viking control of England gradually gave way to the English monarchy under Alfred the Great (871-901), while the Church in Denmark gained increased political power. Denmark's borders expanded following the successful wars of Valdemar II, (the Victorious), who ruled from 1202 to1241. His conquest included southern Sweden, especially Scania, as well as Estonia.

The original structure of Aalborg's Budolfi Kirke was built in the early 12th century.

Thus Denmark was a great empire for this short historic period. Then, as today, the importance of ocean-based trade routes was vital to Denmark's economic survival.

A particularly significant figure during the Valdemar Period was Absalon (1128-1201), who was not a monarch but rather an advisor to King Valdemar I and bore the name of the third son of King David of Israel. Absalon played an important role in both Denmark's religious and military history, and is credited with founding the city of Copenhagen as both a trading and religious center. Church influence had been increasing throughout Denmark, and hundreds of new churches dotted the rolling hills of Jutland, Fyn, and Sealand. A powerful landowner, Absalon was ordained as the Danish Bishop of Roskilde and the Bishop of Scania in southern Sweden. He built one of Denmark's most famous cathedrals at Roskilde where most of the Danish royal families rest in peace.

The Osterlars Church on the Island of Bornholm (c.1160).

Valdemar II instituted several important legal changes, including the Code of Jutland(1241), which applied to most of Denmark and the Scania possessions in Southern Sweden, and the replacement of many of the more primitive laws, such as trial by ordeal.

During the latter period of the Valdemar monarchs, a German trading group, an association of merchants called "The Hanseatic League," evolved into a significant pseudo-monopoly centered in Lubeck, Germany. The league controlled important trading centers in Bergen, Norway and Visby, on the Swedish island of Gotland, and other northern locations. The league dominated the salt trade in Northern Europe, highly important for the preservation of herring since there were four meatless days weekly during the Middle Ages for the believers. Trade in other products such as hemp, lumber and other foodstuffs were also economically vital within the region.

It became the mission of Margrethe (1375-1412), daughter of Valdemar Atterdag, to stem this powerful Hanseatic rival to Danish companies. Following the death of her husband, the Norwegian King Hakon, and her son Olaf, she formed a union of three kingdoms–Norway, Sweden (Scania was already under Danish rule), and Denmark. The union was sealed in the castle at Kalmar in Sweden (then including Finland), extending Denmark's political power into a vast empire that included those three countries and their possessions, such as Greenland and Iceland, the Faroe, Shetland and Orkney islands. The Kalmar Union had a long life, from 1397 to 1523, first under Queen Margrethe I. However, after Margrethe's young son and heir to the throne Olaf died, she became Queen to Norway only, but cleverly managed to convince the powerful nobles that she was the power behind the Kalmar Union. She chose her brother-in-law's son Eric of Pomerania first as her co-regent and ultimately her successor in 1397.

Curbing the economic power of the Hanseatic League and dominating the Baltic Sea lanes was a priority of Eric's. He initiated a long-term policy of collecting a tax, or a Sound Dues, borne by all ships passing Elsinore on Sealand's northern shore. Danish shipping, as well as its economic importance, gradually strengthened and Denmark, along with other countries exploited by the dominance of Hanseatic trade, developed their own economic institutions, contributing to the gradual decline of the league. Other issues facing Eric included the trend in Sweden towards independence from Denmark and the ongoing problem of Schlesvig-Holstein—a complex social and political land dispute with Germany that continued into the 20th century.

Many of the future kings of Denmark faced ongoing conflicts over ownership of both southern Sweden (Scania) and the two regions of Holstein in Germany and Schlesvig, claimed by both Germany and Denmark in various periods. Scania was lost to Denmark during the late Kalmar period from 1521-1523 but was regained temporarily under Christian II (1513-1523). Christian II was a heavy handed-monarch, and not a friend of the nobility in either Sweden or Denmark. An invitation to his dinner party was one that Swedish nobles should have rejected. Following dessert in a castle in Sweden, the king had 82 Swedish nobles executed in a bloodbath in Stockholm's Old Town. Understandably, this annoyed the Swedish nobles and led by Gustav Vasa, Sweden gradually broke away from Danish dominance and strengthened its own monarchy. Several Danish monarchs tried in vain to recapture Scania.

Christian III (1535-1559) was a significant monarch who strengthened the Reformation in Denmark, embracing Lutheranism and adding the former Catholic Church property to his coffers. He also raised the Danish flag, the Dannebrog, over both Schlesvig and Holstein, resuming the ongoing ownership battle.

By the late sixteenth century, when Denmark's most renowned Christian IV (1588-1648) became king, Lutheranism was solidly in place. Danes affectionately remember Christian IV for his architectural innovations. He cultivated the Dutch High Renaissance by bringing French decorative trimmings to Denmark, hence the exciting skyline of Copenhagen where many of the high spires carry his signature. Christian IV built many important namesake buildings in Copenhagen, such as his summer palace Rosenborg; the unique Round Tower; the Bourse, the world's first stock exchange (grain, salt, and herring were important trading commodities); the canals of Christianshavn; residential homes called Nyboder for seamen. He also completed the building of Kronborg Castle and Fredericksborg Castle, both originally built by his father Frederick II. Akershus Castle in Oslo, Norway was another of Christian IV's additions. He was, however, not so renowned for his military and economic skills. Denmark was bankrupt following Christian's frivolous battles against Sweden and her allies in the Thirty Years' War. Christian IV was routed at the Battle of Kolberg Roads and lost many of his Swedish provinces and one eye.

Following the death of Christian IV, his son Frederick III (1648-1670) wore the crown of Denmark. Sweden gradually rose to become a powerful empire during the 17th and early 18th centuries, and Frederick III, although having a superior navy and winning some significant victories, continued to lose Swedish land in wars with Sweden's skilled strategist Charles X, despite help from the Dutch. During the watch of Frederick III, the terms of the Treaty of Roskilde (1658) permanently sealed Swedish ownership of all former Danish land, including the agriculturally fertile provinces of Scania, Halland and Blekinge.

Frederick III did earn his place in Danish history when all classes agreed that the king would rule as an absolute monarch. The absolute monarchy would continue in Denmark until a new constitution and parliamentary democracy was introduced in 1849.

Denmark embarked on several wars with Sweden during the 17th and early 18th centuries. Christian V (1670-1699) was an enlightened leader who innovated changes in Danish laws, the "Danske Lov" or Danish Code, applying them first to Denmark and later to Norway. However, his military talent was not as well-honed and Christian V lost his attempt to regain land during the Scania War (1675-1679) despite help from pro-Danish "guerrilla" fighters. Frederick IV (1699-1730), son of Christian V, also faced a strong, ambitious King Charles XII of Sweden, who made the mistake of taking on the mighty Peter the Great of Russia. Charles XII aspired to rule over most of Northern Europe, including Denmark and Norway. However, Denmark's naval hero Peder Wessel, a.k.a. Tordenskjold, destroyed a large portion of the Swedish fleet, thereby reversing gains made by Charles XII, who eventually died in battle, of a head wound.

The early Danish Vikings ruled over northeastern England. Beginning in the 17th century and to this day, England has been an important trading partner of Denmark. This relationship was challenged during the period of the Napoleonic Wars when Denmark sided with the French. It was under Frederick VI's watch in 1801 that Admiral Lord Nelson shelled Copenhagen without mercy. Danish naval power had been legendary. Fearing that the French would use Danish ships against England, the English Duke of Wellington (whose boots are immortalized as "Wellingtons") was ordered to bomb Copenhagen during the first week of September 1807, completing what the now dead Lord Nelson had started. Danish participation in the war lasted seven years, and by its end in 1814, Denmark had lost much of its fleet to England. Following the complex negotiations between the warring parties, Denmark lost Norway to Sweden (Norway retained self-governing status) and Sweden lost Finland to Russia. The complex question of Schleswig-Holstein was, as always, a muddled mess, with Holstein now a part of the German Confederation. The Danevirke, that extraordinary wall which once defined the northern Danish-German border, became only a curious tourist attraction.

The Schlesvig-Holstein boundary between Germany and Denmark would be decided during the two Schlesvig-Holstein wars from 1849 to 1864 in Fredericia, an otherwise peaceful, geographically important city in Jutland.

King Frederick VII, pressured by his citizens, ended the period of absolute monarchy by signing a new liberal constitution in 1848. Peasants became free citizens and a new two-chamber Parliament replaced the single chamber in Copenhagen. Under the new constitution, Schlesvig would be a permanent Danish possession. This legislation was unacceptable to Prussia and Austria.

Austria allied itself with Prussia in an attempt to gain permanent possession of both Holstein, in Germany, and northern and southern Schlesvig by sending their armies through the Jutland peninsula into the belly of Denmark. After routing the Danes in Holstein, the first of two battles took place in Fredericia, where the Danes outnumbered the invaders and won the initial so-called three-year Schlesvig War in June 1849. This victory is still celebrated in Fredericia. A second war in 1864 favored the Austrian/Prussian armies. The terms of the war gave Holstein, which was already part of the German Federation, and all Schlesvig to Germany. Following other short-term disputes, a plebiscite following WWI in 1920 confirmed Denmark's ownership of northern Schlesvig under the terms of the Treaty of Versailles in June 1919.

Eric of Pomerania enacted the Sound Dues in 1429. Later legislation abolished them in 1857. Kronborg Castle, once identified as the location for enforcing Sound Dues, now became immortalized as one of the world's most beautiful castles where the ghost of the pagan Prince Amlet (a.k.a. the fictional Hamlet) roams its halls to act out his subconscious longings.

Since the mid-19th century Denmark has matured into a modern democracy. Its artists, chefs, philosophers, architects, physicists, politicians, and economists have made global impacts. Visit Skagen in Northern Jutland and marvel at the special light captured by its Golden Age painters, or Odense, birthplace of Denmark's most famous son, Hans Christian Andersen. Copenhagen was home to the world famous sculptor Thordenskjald and the philosopher Soren Kierkegaard. Museums dedicated to the work of modern painters Per Kirkeby and Asger Jorn honor their memory in Jutland. Enjoy the music of Hans Christian Lumbye, Niels Gade, and the choreography of the father of Danish ballet August Bournonville in the Royal Theater or the innovative new opera house in Copenhagen. Special applause to the U.S.-Danish citizen Victor Borge, a U.S. Kennedy Center honoree, whose gentle humor and unique acting and musical skills are universally admired. The list is unending. The arts prospered as urbanization, railroads, and automobiles brought rural residents to the larger cities during the last century. Copenhagen is home to about one-fourth of the Danish population of about five million today, with bicycles and driverless trains adding to the color of the fast-changing landscape.

A word about Danish agriculture. Once the mainstay of the Danish economy, today agriculture represents only about two percent of gross domestic product. The mid-19th century, a period of bleak economic outlook, gave rise to the admirable Danish agricultural cooperatives based on an English movement that unified Danish farmers while also providing them with rural capital. The co-ops enabled farmers, despite their modest unit size, to enjoy the benefits of larger-scale production and distribution. Danish agriculture during the 20th century shifted its production from grains, especially wheat, to livestock and a meat processing industry that sends high-quality butter, cheeses, and pork products to world markets, especially those in Germany, England, and the United States.

Denmark experienced one of its darkest periods in the 20th century during the German occupation. Despite a 1939 non-aggression pact between Germany and Denmark, Hitler invaded in 1940 to use the Jutland seacoast as a military advantage and raid food supplies. Danish resistance was remarkable given the size of the country relative to Hitler's forces—only small pockets of Danes supported Nazi Germany. The occupation was brutal and included burning buildings in Tivoli Park and the East Asiatic Company, and executions of nationals. The Danes saved 99 percent of their Jewish citizens in a historically unique act of massive citizen cooperation throughout the country. The rescue required the cooperation of Danish fishermen using their boats to transport 8,000 Jewish citizens to neutral Sweden. The holy scrolls of the Jewish Bible, the Torah, were also rescued from the synagogue on Krystalgade and transferred secretly to nearby Trinity Church, adjacent to King Christian IV's Round Tower. In the memorial park in Hellerup there is a monument to the 106 resistance members shot by the Germans. The monument features a poem by the resistance poet, Kaj Munk, who was also executed. It reads:

> "Boys, you boys who died,
> You lit for Denmark
> In her darkest gloom
> A brightening dawn."

In recent decades Denmark is proudly a successful Western democracy. Its social legislation is admirable, although financed by relatively high taxes. Denmark is a member of the European Union, NATO, the United Nations, and the Organisation for Economic Co-operation and Development, among other international organizations. Danish troops served alongside American counterparts in many global arenas, including Iraq and Afghanistan. Most Danes admire and respect their royal family members, who are symbols of national solidarity.

Margrethe I, the first queen in the Danish royal lineage, is the namesake of Denmark's present Queen Margrethe II, and both represent the only "ruling" females in the Danish royal hierarchy. The royal families today in Denmark and other European countries are largely symbolic with political power resting in the parliaments.

Queen Margethe II is a renowned artist and her husband, Prince Henric, a talented sculptor. They represent the world's longest continuing monarchy and are beloved by the Danes and respected globally. Several years ago I saw her in the royal carriage with the Japanese Emperor on the world's first motorless walking and shopping streets, Stroget. It was a pleasant personal experience, nearly 50 years after a comical man walked me around Tivoli Park in order to practice his English.

Cityscape of Copenhagen.

The Vikings

A demonstration of Viking cooking over peat in **Borg, Norway**. The Viking diet varied by region, but along the Norwegian coast small arable areas sustained field crops, livestock, berries, and nuts. Fish and other sea life was plentiful as well.

A bridge from the Viking Period on the **Haervejen Trail, Jutland**. Bridges such as these may have been built at the time of Harald Bluetooth during the late 10th century.

Rollo (Rolf), an early Viking chief born c.846, was from the island of **Giske, Norway**, near Alasund. He led Viking settlers to France, settling in Normandy as the First Duke of Normandy.

Honfluer in Normandy, France, was among many Viking hubs settled by Rollo and the Vikings in the 9th century. It is a popular tourist center and boasts one of the most picturesque harbors in France.

Two large runic stones mark the site at **Jelling, Jutland**, where Christianity began in the 9th century. Harald Bluetooth made one stone for his parents, King Gorm and Queen Thyra, which bears an inscription: "King Harald made these runes in memory of Gorm his father and Thyra his mother. Harald who conquered all of Denmark and Norway and made the Danes Christian." The second stone is inscribed: "King Gorm made these runes in memory of his wife Thyra."

Visby, the largest town on the Swedish island of Gotland, had a strong Danish presence from the Viking period until the 17th century. Its geographic importance began as a Viking gateway to Russia and later Visby was the paramount Baltic trading town of the German-based Hanseatic League. Queen Margrethe I of Denmark successfully curbed the monopolistic power of the league in Visby, as did her great-nephew King Eric of Pomerania. Later, both King Frederick II and his son King Christian IV struggled to hold this Baltic trading center but failed and by the mid-17th century Sweden had totally broken away. The beauty of Visby's architecture, its preservation of many ancient churches and fortifications, and its world-famous roses attract shiploads of visitors annually.

The Spiritual Landscape

Absalom, Bishop of Roskilde, is credited with the founding of the city of Copenhagen during the 12th century under King Valdemar I to protect Denmark's trade and establish an important religious center. His bronze equestrian statue overlooks **Hojbro Square** near Christiansborg Palace and the historic Gammel Strand area.

The 12th-century **Viborg Domkirke, in the city of Viborg** in north-central Jutland, was the site of early coronation ceremonies and an important center of the Danish Reformation led by the monk Hans Tavsen.
Viborg was established as a bishopric in the 11th century.

Interior view of the **Viborg Domkirke**. Wall frescoes and light fittings by the renowned Danish painter Joakim Skovgaard add to the significance of the cathedral.

View of the **town of Ribe** from the steeple lookout of the Domkirke (pg. 30). Archbishop Ansgar built Denmark's first church in Ribe in 862 A.D. on or near this site, elevating Ribe as an important bishopric of the Holy Roman Empire. Ribe, one of Denmark's oldest cities, was a significant 9th-century trading center. The Romanesque Domkirke was restored during the late 18th century.

The **Osterlars Church on the Island of Bornholm** (c.1160) typifies the unique round church design and is one of Denmark's finest and most charming Romanesque buildings.

Aalborg's Budolfi Kirke was originally built in the early 12th century
with many additions and restorations initiated over the years.
It's engaging Baroque spire was added in 1780.

"Church of Our Saviour"
(Vor Frelsers Kirke, 1696)
in Christianshavn,
a suburb of Copenhagen,
is identifiable by
the unique steeple
added in 1752.

Copenhagen's Helligaandskirken (portal detail) was originally built as an Augustinian monastery during the 13th century. It was restored following a destructive fire in 1728. Its decorative portals are among the most famous in Northern Europe.

The city of Roskilde was an important Viking settlement and former
medieval capital of Denmark. **The Roskilde Cathedral** (left) contains
many chapels that hold the final final resting places of Danish monarchs,
including Queen Margrethe I (above) and Christian IV.

King Christian IV and the Royal Landscape

The castle at Kalmar, Sweden, was the site of the signing of the Kalmar Union agreement
giving the Danish Queen Margrethe I and later her grand-nephew Eric of Pomerania
control over all the Nordic countries. The Kalmar Union dissolved during King Eric's watch
due to his unpopular ambitions to increase his power in Sweden
while the momentum towards Swedish nationalism was rising under the Vasa family.

The Gavno Estate (photo illustration) in South Sealand was first
purchased by Queen Margrethe I in 1398 as a Dominican convent.
A titled landowner named Count Otto Thott bought this well-placed
property not far from Copenhagen in the early 18th century.
Today the estate attracts tourists to its important art
and library collection and unique tulip garden.

Rosenborg Castle in Copenhagen was the summer palace of King Christian IV and is a Dutch Renaissance gem. Christian lived at Rosenborg with his second wife Kirsten Munk, Countess of Schlesvig-Holstein. During her marriage to the king she gave birth to 12 children of which the first 11 were his.

King Christian IV's crown at Rosenborg Castle. Christian IV
is remembered largely for his architectural innovations—and
the second verse of the Danish national anthem, which places him
on a lofty mast of his ship, bravely facing the Swedish enemy.
Unspoken was the economic disaster that resulted from
Christian's decision to enter the Thirty Years' War,
which left Denmark bankrupt.

King Christian IV built the harbor town of **Christianshavn**,
between Copenhagen and Amager Island from 1618 to 1623
both for defensive reasons and to increase shipping capacity.

King Christian IV's Bourse in Copenhagen was one of the world's first stock exchanges and used as such until the mid-19th century. It is identifiable by its spire consisting of four intertwined dragons.

Photo illustration (right) shows view
of Kronborg Castle from the sea.

Kronborg Castle (site of the original Krogen Castle) in North Sealand at Elsinore is where Sound Dues–introduced by Eric of Pomerania–were collected and where the ghost of Shakespeare's Hamlet wanders. The present Renaissance-era castle was built by King Frederick II, father of Christian IV, during the late 16th century and used during his war with Sweden. King Christian IV did extensive repairs to Kronborg following a fire in 1629. Additional repairs to Kronborg were undertaken by King Frederick III following the Swedish bombing in 1658.

The home of the wealthy merchant **Jens Bang** was built in Aalborg during the reign
of King Christian IV and is one of the finest 17th-century Renaissance buildings of its kind.

King Christian IV built the large **Valdemar Estate** on Funen in the mid-17th century. It was named for his youngest son who was killed in battle and never lived to reside at the property. The Danish naval hero Admiral Niels Juul later made the estate his home, now a public museum and restaurant.

The charming Pavilion of the Valdemar Estate.

Christian IV's northern Kingdom of Norway was ruled from his **Castle Akerhus in Oslo**.
The Norwegian tall ship, the **Christian Radich**, is docked in the foreground.

King Christian IV built the **Round Tower** in 1640 as an observatory, part of a project which later included the adjacent Trinitis Church and University of Copenhagen buildings. Following a dispute between the noted astronomer **Tycho Brahe** and the king, Brahe moved to the island of Hven and a new observatory called Uranienborg. Later, Brahe became the official astronomer for the Bohemian King and Holy Roman Emperor Rudolph II.

This modern planetarium was built on a man-made lake in central Copenhagen and named for the renowned Danish astronomer **Tycho Brahe**.

The Road to Democracy

"The Horse" is the popular nickname for the equestrian statue of King Christian V, who developed the area into a beautiful public park called **Kongens Nytorv**, the King's New Market in the center of Copenhagen. Ironically, Christian V was a somber pietist and his statue stands before the old Royal Theater.

The enthusiastic builder Christian V constructed the main guardhouse of the **Royal Naval Station** (left) on a secured base in Copenhagen. Christian V, son of Frederick III, Denmark's first absolute monarch, formalized his father's policies in legislation called "The Danish Law."

Kongens Nytorv (below) is a popular park for relaxation. The gentleman seems distracted from the historic significance of one of Europe's oldest equestrian statues.

Graduates of Denmark's Gymnasium celebrate each year by dancing around Christian V (above) in this well-visited location in Kongens Nytorv. Danes have a special affection towards **"The Horse"** and its rider despite his loss of Swedish land during the Scanian Wars.

Amalienborg Palace became the royal residence following a fire,
which destroyed Christiansborg Palace in 1794. Amalienborg consists of four buildings
and has been the home to the royal family since King Christian VII (1766-1806).

The **statue of King Frederick V** [1746-1766] holds court in the center of Amalienborg Palace surrounded by the royal residences of the residing monarch Queen Margrethe II and her husband Prince Henrik. Frederick V, far less puritanical than his father, revived cultural life in Denmark. The statue, sculpted by French artist Jacques Saly, took 30 years to complete.

Christiansborg Palace, on **Christiansborg Slotsplads**, is the home of the Danish one-chamber Parliament. The Palace was first built by King Christian VI but was destroyed by several fires. The present building was completed in 1928.

The statue of a Danish rifleman, **"The Valiant Footsoldier," by H.V. Bisen** became the symbol of Fredericia and is the world's first statue dedicated to an unknown soldier.

The statue of **King Frederick VII** stands before Christiansborg palace. King Frederick VII ruled during the Slesvig Wars (1848-1850), which defined Denmark's border with Germany. This king was the last ruler of the Oldenburg dynasty. He was an enlightened king and replaced the 190-year absolute monarchy with a liberal constitution, which called for democratically elected representation in a two-chambered parliament.

A memorial relief honors the fallen soldiers of the **battle of Fredericia** in 1849. Danish forces won an initial victory over the combined Austrian-Prussian Holsteiners but suffered large casualties.

The town of **Fredericia** (Latin for Frederick) lies in the center of Denmark in Jutland, and not far from the German border. It was originally built as a fortress town. Fredericia served as a major battleground during the late 19th-century Schlesvig Wars between Denmark and the Austrian-Prussian alliance.

Danes enjoy a colorful parade and other festivities each year to commemorate the Danish victory over the Austrian-Prussian armies in 1849 and the beginning of constitutional democracy.

A **Jewish cemetery**, established in 1709, is a national historic preservation in Fredericia. The king granted the right of asylum and freedom of worship to Jews and other persecuted groups, including French Huguenots, in 1682

Denmark's official state religion is Lutheranism, however,
Denmark has traditionally supported free religious expression.
The **Copenhagen Synagogue** was dedicated on April 12, 1833.
It's Torah scrolls (the Jewish Bible) were hidden from Nazi destruction
in nearby Trinity Church, adjacent to the Round Tower.

Fredericia as seen from the town's fortifications originally built by King Frederick III
in the mid-17th century as Danes prepared for war with Sweden.

Views of the old section of Fredericia.

Two views of a unique cooperative housing facility called **Solvang in the Erritso District, Fredericia**. Residents own condominium-style town houses and share a common, temperature-controlled indoor center street (seen at right), dining rooms, gardens, guest chambers and showers, and other amenities. This cooperative lifestyle was mimicked in similar projects in the United States, notably California.

An interior view of "the street" in the cooperative housing facility Solvang in Fredericia.

The Maritime Landscape

The *Danmark*

The *Danmark* played a significant role in the maritime history of the United States. In 1939 the *Danmark* was on a routine training cruise in the United States when World War II broke out. The captain at that time, Knud Hansen, was informed that Germany had invaded Denmark. Consequently, the *Danmark* remained in the United States serving as a training ship for U.S. sailors. The first officer of the *Danmark*, Knud Langevard, not only supervised the training of 5,000 U.S. sailors but also convinced U.S. authorities of the value of learning basic seamanship aboard a tall ship.

Following the war, the U.S. Coast Guard obtained the *Eagle* from Germany as part of a reparation agreement. Reflecting this special kinship between the two ships, the *Danmark* sails as the first ship behind the *Eagle* in official tall ship parades.

The *Danmark* moored in Washington, D.C., where it hosted receptions for U.S. members of Congress, diplomats and friends of the Danish Community.

"Bottoms Up–The *Danmark*" is an unmanipulated photograph of the ship
docked in the harbor in Washington, D.C.
Had I chosen red wine no photograph would have been possible!

Left. Denmark's important naval tradition is preserved through its internationally recognized tall ship, the *Danmark*. The 77-meter (252-foot) training ship is shown at its Frederikshavn port in Jutland where male and female cadets ages 17 to 21 board for an annual training cruise. The *Danmark* is a fully rigged three-mast ship holding 80 cadets and a 15-person crew.

Above. The *Danmark* moored in Copenhagen at the A.P. Moeller/Maersk A/S headquarters. Moeller/Maersk is one of the world's largest shipping companies and finances many of the *Danmark's* training activities.

The *Danmark* is a purely educational training ship where male and female cadets learn important maritime skills to give them a head start towards a naval or commercial career. Classes include navigation, seamanship, sail repair, and a variety of related academic courses. The cadets prepare all meals during the training period.

Right. Cadets fearlessly master the 2,000 meters (over 6,500 feet) of standing rig and 26 sails following rigorous training in ship safety.

A sailor, a sail, and the sea.

Above. **Captain Vilhelm Hansen** served as captain of the *Danmark* from 1964-1986. He is shown at the helm of the *Danmark* during the final minutes of his career, steering the ship into the South Street Seaport in New York at the close of Operation Sail - A Salute to Liberty in 1986. Hansen was a well-known figure in various U.S. ports, enhancing the *Danmark's* reputation as a floating embassy as well as a training ship. He received many honors in the United States, including the Danish-American Society Man of the Year Award and the National Maritime Historical Society's Walter Cronkite Award for Excellence in Maritime Education. A tribute to Captain Hansen was recorded in the U.S. Senate Congressional Record, June 14, 2000.

Left. **Captain Kurt Andersen**, shown at the helm in Frederikshavn, has been the Master of the *Danmark* since 2000.

The *Danmark* under sail

The *Danmark* under sail

The *Danmark* under sail

World-class Danish comedian and musician **Victor Borge** demonstrates
his nautical skills at the helm of the *Danmark* during
Operation Sail – A Salute to Liberty in 1986.

Left. **Captain Vilhelm Hansen** waves at the Mexican Tall Ship the *Cuahtemac* during the Manhattan leg of the Parade of Tall Ships on July 4, 1986.

Below. The image of the Twin Towers, taken from the *Danmark* during the Parade of Tall Ships, took on a deeper meaning as a memorial to those lost in the tragedy of Sept. 11, 2001.

The Eagle

The 295-foot *Eagle* is the official training ship of the U.S. Coast Guard and carries 180 trainees. German built, the *Eagle* was acquired under a reparation agreement following World War II. The *Danmark* traditionally follows the *Eagle* in U.S.-based official parades, such as such as Operation Sail - A Salute to Liberty on July 4, 1986.

Frigate Jylland

The museum ship, the Frigate *Jylland*, moored at Ebeltoft in Jutland, is said to be the world's largest wooden ship at 71 meters (232 feet). It was a formidable warhorse against the Austrian-Prussian forces during the Schlesvig wars, notably the Battle of Helgoland under the command of Admiral Niels Juhl. The Danes won the naval victory but lost the war.

Danish Modern

Hans Christian Andersen

Hans Christian Andersen was born in Odense, Fyn in April 1805, the son of a poor shoemaker and an uneducated washerwoman. Although this gifted Danish artist gave the world novels, poems, a travel guide, and even an opera—more than 150 works in all—he is best remembered for his timeless fairy tales about little match girls, mermaids, teapots, ugly ducklings, and animated shadows—84 tales written just as much for adults as children. He didn't invent the "fairy tale" but was the first to put words into the mouths of everyday objects—and those stories had a dark side as well. Andersen believed that a loving God would guide him to success, and so it was. He was invited to the royal palaces throughout Europe, met with great literary figures such as Charles Dickens, Heinrich Heine and Victor Hugo and courted the "Swedish Nightingale" Jenny Lind—very innocently. He never married but was content to receive the admiration and applause of the masses throughout Europe. Andersen wasn't a journalist in the formal sense, but his tales often described poorly qualified rulers and irresponsible governments. In "The Emperor's New Clothes," the incompetent king couldn't see that he was completely naked during his coronation. In "The Shadow," Andersen illustrates the dangers of totalitarianism through a shadow becoming independent from its owner and eventually ruling both the individual and the entire society. The tale "Auntie Toothache" describes a country where everything dies and ends up as trash. Of course many stories had happy endings—after trials and tribulations. In "The Ugly Duckling" Andersen convinced his young audiences that with insight one could see the beauty in every creature. That's why Andersen is universally loved and admired. He brings a fresh perspective to express complicated adult observations and offers hope to readers everywhere. Don't take the word of a roaming photographer. Visit the harbor side of Langelinie in Copenhagen, walk the long promenade to the evocative sculpture of the Little Mermaid, and look at the faces of some of the millions of tourists from the world over who make the same pilgrimage to see the lonely lady looking northwards towards the open sea.

A statue of **Hans Christian Andersen** sits in the Town Hall Square in Copenhagen, one of many of Denmark's favorite son, including statues at his birthplace in Odense and in the King's Garden at Rosenborg Castle.

Andersen lived and wrote several works at No. 67 on the Nyhavn Canal, close to the Royal Theater on Kongens Nyhavn (The King's New Square). He had hoped to perform at the theater but was rejected.

Andersen could look from his apartment on to the busy Nyhavn canal in a neighborhood filled with the sounds of small craft and colorful bars and cafes.

The original **Royal Theater** in Copenhagen was commissioned by King Frederick V on Kongens Nytorv in 1748 as a comedy house. The present building was erected in 1872 and opened its doors to serious theater in 1874 and is the original home of the world famous Danish Royal Ballet. My first visit to this grand temple of the arts was in 1959 to see the Royal Ballet perform classical Bourneville creations such as *Napoli*. King Frederick IX and Queen Ingrid were in attendance along with their guests, the King and Queen of Greece. The ticket price was approximately $1, a bit less that the $2 paid for a steak dinner at the then nearby ABC Cafeteria.

This "portrait" of the original **Little Mermaid** sculpture was taken in 1959.
A few years later thieves removed her head, which was subsequently replaced.
The Danish police treated the crime as a homicide. The statue is one of the
world's most-visited tourist attractions.

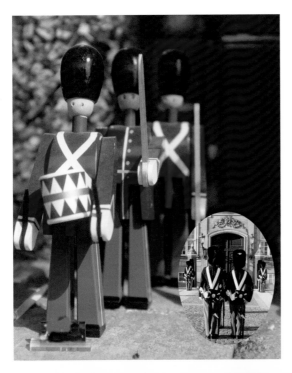

Wooden soldiers by K. Bojesen.
Insert: Photo of the Royal King's Guards at
Amelienborg Palace. H.C. Andersen described
the guards in "The Staunch Tin Soldiers":
"...each soldier was the very image of the other.
They wore splendid red tunics with blue trousers."

This image, taken on a farm in Jutland, proves everything has its limits. As H.C. Andersen wrote in "The Marsh King's Daughter": "This is too terrible. But now tell me—what happened after that?"

A clever young man on Stroget, Copenhagen's walking street, dips his hand in the "cookie jar" owned by a street entertainer.

Danish revelers participate in a Nordic Mardi Gras in Copenhagen.

A performer dressed as a chimney sweep entertains tourists on Stroget. Andersen wrote in "The Shepherdess and the Chimney Sweep": "He was as just and trim and tidy as anyone else, for he only pretended to be a chimney sweep!

An apprentice chimney sweep!

Two members of the clergy enjoy an ice cream date in Copenhagen.

A Danish senior citizen finds his happiness with a tasty ice cream cone in Tivoli Park.

Tivoli contains prize-winning gardens, fine restaurants, and carnival rides. Each night during the summer buildings such as the Nimb Hotel add a fairy-tale ambience to the Copenhagen skyline.

Tivoli Park in central Copenhagen was the brainchild of George Carstensen in 1843.
Its free Chinese-style pantomime theater often features dancers from the Royal Ballet
during the summer.

Harlequin courts lovely Columbine in a staging of *Pierrot* at the pantomime theater in Tivoli Park.

A picturesque postcard view of Tivoli at dusk.

The **Nimb Hotel**, known as the Nimb, is a five-star boutique hotel.

One of the buildings comprising the **University of Copenhagen** was built
in 1835 in the Classical architectural style. This section of the university
is located in the so-called Latin Quarter of Copenhagen.

The dramatic **Gefion Fountain** is a powerful creation by Anders Bundgaard on the Langelinie promenade near the waterfront. It tells the story of Nordic goddess Gefion with her four oxen sons who were responsible for the creation of Denmark's Sealand from Swedish territory.

Very few of these ornamental kiosks remain in Copenhagen. Reminders of the late 19th and early 20th centuries, they now function as small clock towers and handy shops for newspapers and snacks.

Above. The noble statue of **King Christian IX** [1863-1906] immortalizes Denmark's first monarch of the House of Glucksburg. Although the temporary loss of territory during the Schlesvig-Holstein war darkened his watch, he enabled more modern social legislation.

Left. The equestrian statue of **King Christian X** is located on St. Anne's Place near the waterfront. King Christian inspired the Danes by firmly opposing German legislation against Jews and other Danish minorities during the WWII occupation. The king proudly rode through the streets of Copenhagen as a symbol of Danish opposition to the occupation

My archival photograph from 1959 captured the mix of electric trams and bicycles
in Copenhagen near the Bourse and Christiansborg Palace.

Amalienborg replaced Christiansborg Palace as a royal residence following a devastating fire in 1794. Amalienborg consists of several mansions within walking distance of the Marble Church (seen in the background) and is designed in the Classical style.

Small homes, many half-timbered or red tiled with grass roofs, add romantic charm throughout Denmark. Many were built during the 18th and early 19th century in small rural towns.

This small town hall in **Dragor**, a suburb of Copenhagen, was once used for local political meetings. According to a tongue-in-cheek legend its twisted chimney was built to prevent political opponents from spying.

This 1846 red forge building (top left), originally from Orback, was photographed at Denmark's
Open Air Museum in Friland using an impressionist manipulation.
Small homes were built to accommodate a growing merchant or middle class.
Doorways seemed to reflect a shorter Danish population in earlier times.

Homes facing the sea in Skagen, Jutland.

19th-Century Denmark

The 19th century brought remarkable changes to the social and economic history of Denmark. The industrial revolution crossed the North Sea from England and resulted in rails replacing horse-drawn wagons. The urban centers grew as rural populations migrated to the major cities, notably Copenhagen. Falling grain prices induced a transition from a grain to a livestock-based agricultural economy. The Folk High Schools, started by Bishop Grundvig, enabled the masses to enjoy an education, and around 1850 a unique cooperative movement began enabling small farmers to enjoy shared capital and a more efficient marketing system. Denmark fought its last war in 1869. Once a great power, Denmark, having lost its possessions, was destined to assume a less dramatic military role—trade and international agreements replacing the battlefield politics.

By the late 19th century social legislation and reforms, common throughout Europe and generated by the Enlightenment, resulted in a democratic, egalitarian society. The absolute monarchy had been abolished; peasants were free and no longer bound to a large, aristocratic landowner. A free press was established, and a democratic political society was born.

The 19th century also saw a flowering of the arts. Hans Christian Andersen arrived in Copenhagen from Odense as a penniless dreamer, and by the time of his death in 1875, became a world famous author of fairy tales, short stories, and novels—honored by royalty throughout the Continent. His colleagues Soren Kierkegaard and Thorvaldsen, the former an innovative religious philosopher and the latter a brilliant sculptor, were both renowned throughout Europe. Painters flocked to Skagen in northern Jutland with its "special light," giving birth to a distinctive national school of painting. These Skagen artists included Christoffer Wilhelm Eckersberg, Anna and Michael Ancher, P.S. Kroyer, Christian Krough, Holger Drachman and others. August Bourneville's ballet music and dance still are favorite programs in the repertoires of the Royal Danish Ballet. It was a remarkable century and its historic events live on in the soul of Denmark and virtually all aspects of its national life.

The 19th-century Skagen painters and poets often met at the **Brondums Hotel**, originally a shop
owned by the father of the famed Danish artist Anna Ancher. She and her husband Michael Ancher were members
of the distinguished community of Skagen painters composed of Holger Drachman, Christoffer Eckersberg,
Vilhelm Hammershoi, Viggo Johansen, P.S. Kroyer, Christian Krohg, and Laurits Tuxen.
Anna Ancher's works reflected the restricted and isolated position of women in 19th-century Danish society.
Michael's works were detailed representations of the local fishermen.

Portrait of **Holgar Drachman** by P.S. Kroyer (The Skagen Museum).
Photograph by the author taken at the National Museum
of Women in the Arts, Washington, D.C. in February 2013.

Opposite.
The closet of Skagen painter
and poet Holgar Drachman.

117.

Two forms of transportation on the beach in Skagen.

German gun bunkers were installed on the beaches of Northern Jutland during the occupation
to prevent allied ships from entering the Kattegat.

Left. The "Nazis" shown here were Danish actors making a film about the occupation in Copenhagen. The setting was so realistic that one passerby fainted in disbelief that the Germans had returned.

The Danish single-chamber Parliament (Folketinget) replaced the two-chamber model under a new 1953 constitution.

Agriculture

Denmark is a low-lying country, its rural rolling hills graced with bright yellow crops of rapeseed. There has been a continual decline in the number of farms in Denmark, although average size has risen and they are more efficient and specialized.

Agriculture was grain based until the 19th century, when a shift occurred towards exporting livestock products, especially in the pig and dairy sectors. Barley remains an important grain and is used as a pig feed. Rye also is an important ingredient in the traditional "snaps" or aquavit. One breed of hog is the Landrace, genetically altered to have an extra rib cage—and hence more bacon. Pig meat and butter exports are supported by healthy farm subsidies provided by Denmark's membership in the European Union.

Top left. The elongated Danish Landrace Hog.

Near left. Daily "life" in a Danish slaughterhouse in Jutland.

124.

Danes of all ages and backgrounds have one thing in common: the bicycle!
Although modern Copenhagen has its share of traffic problems,
more commuters have begun hopping on bicycles to avoid high fuel prices
and road congestion. Usage has risen but not to 1960 levels when
there were about 500,000 bicycles used in Copenhagen. A new subway is
under construction.

Interior view of the Central Railroad Terminal in Copenhagen,
a hub for connections throughout Denmark and continental Europe.

Exterior view of **Aalborg's** railroad terminal. By the
late 19th century, rail lines were expanded throughout Denmark,
opening up areas such as Jutland to tourists and merchants.

An S-Tog (local) train station in central Copenhagen.

Two views of the postmodern
Copenhagen Opera House,
centrally located on the harbor
across from Amalienborg Palace.
Designed by Henning Larsen,
it opened in 2005 and holds
about 1,500 seats.

The Carl-Henning Pedersen and Else Alfel Museum in Herning, Jutland. Pedersen (1913-2007)
was a member of the 20th-century COBRA group, along with the Dane Ansgar Jorn
and other prominent European artists. The work was recognized for its freedom of line,
form and color, often using figures from a child-like dream world.

Left. An avant-garde view of Chairman Mao by Andy Warhol at Denmark's modern museum, **Louisiana** in Humlebaek, North Sealand.

Below. A curious viewer at the **Glyptotek Museum** in Copenhagen.

The **Ny Carlsberg Glyptotek** located near Tivoli houses a world-class collection of mixed media from Classical sculptures to exhibitions of the modern masters.

Author, poet, and educator **Poul Borum** (1934-1996) agreed
to one photograph in 1992 while enjoying an otherwise
reflective moment in Copenhagen's Kranapolski Café.

Famed author **Isak Dinesen** (a.k.a. Karen Blixen)
returned from her life in Nairobi, Kenya,
to the family estate in Humlebaek, now a museum.

Right. World famous-musician-comedian
Victor Borge at Ribild Park in 1987 where
the American Fourth of July is celebrated annually.

Thousands of Danes fill the hills of **Rebild Park** to celebrate the July 4th American holiday. Denmark was among the first European nations to recognize American independence and the only country to annually celebrate the historic anniversary.

Margrethe II, Queen Regent of Denmark, and **Hendrik, Prince Consort of Denmark,** represent the country at the Rebild festivities each year. (1987 photograph)

Queen Margrethe II is often seen riding through Copenhagen for official visits as shown here on the walking street Stroget with the Japanese Emperor Akihito.

A young lady enjoys playing the role of queen at a Tivoli Park parade.

Addendum

Danish Rulers

Gorm the Old	c.936 – c.958	King of a United Denmark
Harald Bluetooth	958 – 985	Introduced Christianity to Denmark
Sven Forkbeard	985 – 1014	
Harald	1014 – 1018	
Canute the Great	1018 – 1035	Conquered England
Hardicanute	1035 – 1042	
Magnus the Good	1042 – 1047	
Sven Estridon	1047 – 1074	Christianity now rooted in society
Harald Hen	1074 – 1080	
Canute the Holy	1080 – 1086	Enlarged Danish Fleet; Murdered in Odense
Olaf Hunger	1086 – 1095	
Eric Egode	1095 – 1103	
Niels	1104 – 1137	
Eric Lamb	1137 – 1146	
Sven Grathe, Canute	1146 – 1157	
Valdemar I, The Great	1157 – 1182	Defeats the Wends
Canute VI	1182 – 1202	Defeats Dukes of Pomerania
Valdemar II, The Victorious	1202 – 1241	Conquered Estonia, Holstein
Eric Ploughpenny	1241 – 1250	
Abel	1250 – 1252	
Christopher I	1252 – 1259	
Eric Clipping	1259 – 1286	
Eric Menved	1280 – 1319	
Christopher II	1320 – 1326 1330 – 1332	
Valdemar Atterdag	1340 – 1375	First Danish Laws; Father of Queen Margrethe
Olaf	1375 – 1387	
Margrethe I	1387 – 1412	United Nordic Countries (Kalmar Union)
Eric of Pomerania	1412 – 1439	Replaced Margrethe I as king; Ruled Kalmar Union
Christopher of Bavaria	1439 – 1448	

DANISH RULERS
HOUSE OF THE OLDENBURG DYNASTY

Christian I	1448 – 1481	United Schlesvig and Holstein
Hans	1481 – 1513	
Christian II	1513 – 1523	Conquered Sweden; Massacred Swedish Nobles
Frederick I	1523 – 1533	
Christian III	1535 – 1559	Introduced Reformation to Denmark
Frederick II	1559 – 1588	
Christian IV	1588 – 1648	Architect King; Entered Thirty Years' War
Frederick III	1648 – 1670	First absolute monarch
Christian V	1670 – 1699	Replaced old Valdemar Statute with "The Danish Laws"
Frederick IV	1699 – 1730	
Christian VI	1730 – 1746	
Frederick V	1746 – 1766	
Christian VII	1766 – 1808	
Frederick VI	1808 – 1839	Seven Years' War 1807-1814 Created Provincial Assemblies
Christian VIII	1839 – 1848	
Frederick VII	1848 – 1863	First Constitutional Monarch First Schlesvig-Holstein War (1848-1850)

HOUSE OF GLUCKSBURG DYNASTY

Christian IX	1863 – 1906	Treaty of Vienna Denmark loses rights to Schlesvig/Holstein
Frederick VIII	1906 – 1912	
Christian X	1912 – 1947	North Schlesvig encorporated Into Denmark inspiration during WW II by riding horseback daily in Copenhagen
Frederick IX	1947 – 1972	
Margrethe II	1972 –	Denmark joins European Union and many international organizations; Voted Happiest Nation in 2013

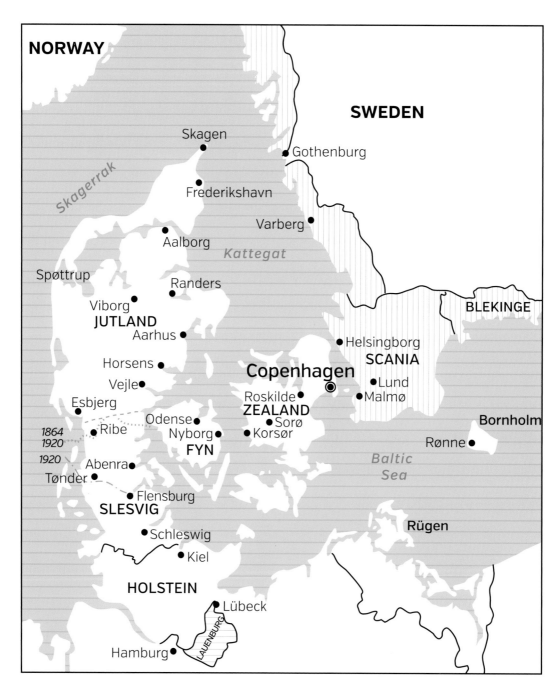

The dotted lines show the new frontiers from 1864 to 1920 when North Shlesvig above Tonder became part of Denmark. The former Danish province of Scania and the North German duchy of Holstein is also shown.
(Source: *Denmark*. W.Glyn Jones. Ernest Benn, Ltd.)

SELECTED BIBLIOGRAPY

Anderson, Robert T. Denmark, *Success of a Developing Nation*. Cambridge, Mass.: Schenkman Publishing Co., 1975.

Arbman, Holger. *The Vikings*. New York: Frederick A, Praeger, 1961.

Brondsted, Johannes. *The Vikings*. London: Penguin Books, 1960.

Clissold, Stephen. Denmark, *The Land of Hans Andersen*. London: Hutchinson and Co., 1956.

Cohen, Marshall H. *Denmark in the European Community: A Decade of Agricultural Change*. Washington: United States. Dept. of Agriculture, 1986.

Faber, Tobias. *A History of Danish Architecture*. Copenhagen: Det Danske Selscab, 1963.

Jacobsen, Helga Seidelin. *An Outline History of Denmark*. Copenhagen: Host and Son, 1986.

Jones, W. Glyn. *Denmark*. London: Ernest Benn Limited, 1970.

Jones, W. Glyn and Gade, Kirsten. *Denmark, The Blue Guide*. London and New York: A and C Black and WW Norton, 1997.

Jones, Gwyn. *A History of the Vikings*. London and New York: Oxford University Press, 1969.

Klindt-Jensen, *Ole. Denmark, Before the Vikings*. London: Thames and Hudson, 1957.

Lauring, Palle. *A History of Denmark.* Copenhagen: Host and Son, 1960.

Lauring, Palle. *A History of Denmark in Pictures*. Denmark: Steen Hasselbalchs Forlag, 1963.

Oakley, Stewart. *The Story of Denmark*. London: Faber and Faber, 1972.

Olesen, Peter and Rasmussen, Peter Bak. *Copenhagen Curiosities*. Copenhagen: Borgens Forlag, 1991.

Royal Danish Ministry of Foreign Affairs. *Denmark, An Official Handbook*. Copenhagen: various years.

Soderberg, Bengt G. *Visby, A Journey Through the Centuries*. Visby: Cop. Gotlandskonst AB, 1960.

Witkowska, Monica and Hald Joanna. *Denmark, Eyewitness Travel*. London, New York, 2010.

Wourinen, John H. *Scandinavia*. New Jersey: Prentice-Hall, 1965.

Virtually all Danish museums and several churches and historic sites have excellent catalogues and handouts which were useful sources of information.

ADDITIONAL PHOTO CAPTIONS

Page 2.
The dramatic sculpture "**Man Meets the Sea II**" by artist Svend Wiig Hansen (1995) symbolizes the historic relationship between Danes and the sea from Viking days to the present. Located on the shores of Esberg, a major shipping port in Jutland, it may be seen by incoming ships for miles as they approach Denmark's friendly shores.

Page 6.
A decorative building address in Copenhagen

Page 8.
Skagan

Page 10.
Road in Jutland

Page 12.
Danish soldier

Page 13.
An organ grinder in the the Aarhus City Center

Page 18.
Reformation Monument, *Bishop Hans Tavsen and the Council of Nobles.* Copenhagen.

Page 19.
Copenhagen at dusk

Page 20.
Button from the uniform
of a Royal Guard

Page 21.
Children at Tivoli

Page 22.
Tivoli

Page 23.
Danish sailors

Page 30.
The steeple of the Ribe
Domkirke

Page 40.
Rosenberg Castle

Page 54.
A view of the statue of
King Frederick V through
the Grecian Ioni columns
at the southern entrance
to Amalienborg Palace

Page 68.
Danmark masthead

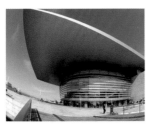

Page 86.
Copenhagen Opera House